THE CALLIGRAPHY BOOK

Peter Grislis

ASHTON SCHOLASTIC
Sydney Auckland New York Toronto London

Grislis, Peter,

The calligraphy book.
ISBN 0 86896 421 2.
1. Calligraphy — Juvenile literature. 1. Title
745.6′1

First published in 1988 by Ashton Scholastic Pty Limited (Inc. in NSW), PO Box 579, Gosford 2250.
Also in Brisbane, Melbourne, Adelaide, Perth and Auckland, NZ.

Photography by Ken Dolling
Typeset by David Graphic Sales Pty Ltd, Sydney
Printed by Griffin Press Ltd, Adelaide

12 11 10 9 8 7 6 5 4 3 2 89/80/9

CONTENTS

BY THESE WORDS LET IT BE KNOWN THAT THIS BOOK IS THE PURCHASED PROPERTY OF THE ONE WHO HAS EXCHANGED GOLD FOR THE GUARDIANSHIP OF ITS SECRETS. SHOULD YOU LAY UNLAWFUL HANDS UPON THIS BOOK EITHER TO BORROW OR STEAL OR OTHERWISE MISAPPROPRIATE SAID BOOK UNDERSTAND THAT THESE CONSEQUENCES SHALL FOLLOW AS NIGHT FOLLOWS DAY. YOUR NOSE WILL ITCH UNBEARABLY WHEN THE URGE TO WRITE IS UPON YOU. YOUR FINGERS WILL PERSPIRE MAKING YOUR QUILL SLIPPERY, THE INK WILL BLEED ACROSS THE PAGE AND THERE WILL BE NO POSITION ON A CHAIR IN WHICH YOUR MISERABLE BONES WILL FIND COMFORT. BUT SHOULD YOU RETURN THIS BOOK UNSCATHED TO ITS RIGHTFUL OWNER THE SYMPTOMS WILL CEASE. THE SUN WILL COME OUT FROM BEHIND ITS CLOUD & A LASTING PEACE WILL ENTER YOUR HEART. RICHES WILL BE SHOWERED ON YOU FROM UNEXPECTED SOURCES & SUCCESS WILL ACCOMPANY ALL YOUR ENDEAVOURS. SO GIVE BACK THE BOOK AND BUY YOUR VERY OWN COPY TO ENJOY.

WHAT IS CALLIGRAPHY?

Calligraphy is beautiful handwriting. We use it to add that extra touch to a letter for someone special, to liven up an invitation, as decoration on a poster, for a unique title page in a book or to really make school assignments come to life. By choosing the correct writing style and arranging the letters in an attractive way we can transform an ordinary page of writing into a lively display. Calligraphy isn't just a matter of 'a flick of the wrist' — it *does* take a bit of practice but it's not as difficult as you might think.

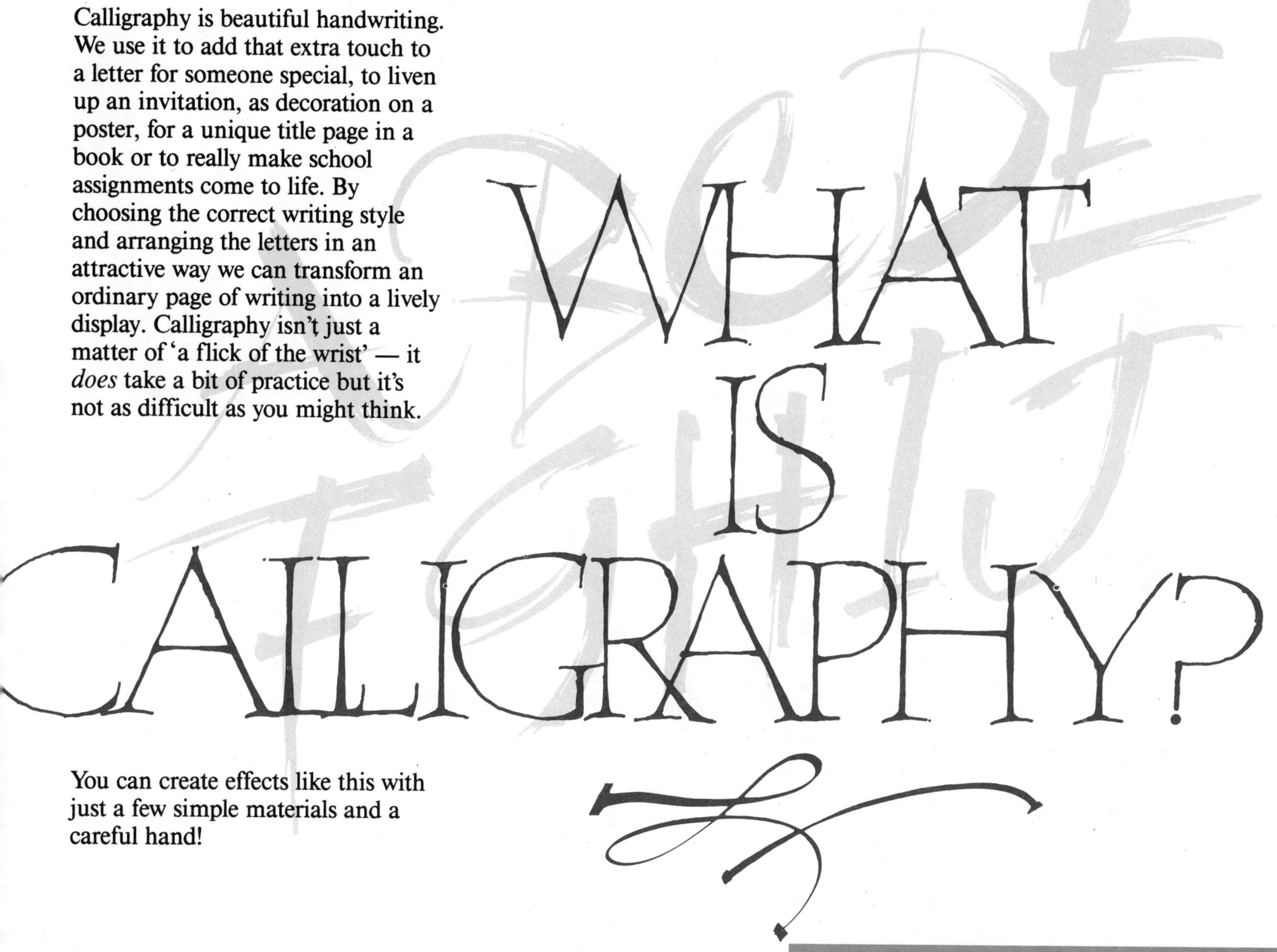

You can create effects like this with just a few simple materials and a careful hand!

The art of
Calligraphy
Calligraphy.
The art of beautiful writing;
a script, usually cursive, although some
times angular produced chiefly by brush,
esp. Chinese, Japanese, or Arabic writing of high aesthetice value.
Line or a group of lines that
either are derived from or resemble
letter forms and are characterized
by qualities usually associated with
cursive writing.

Certificate
of Merit
Awarded to
John Smith-Douglas.
D Monte
Signed
6/8/89
Dated

PERSONALISED WRAPPING PAPER

Look at the fun you will be able to have with pen, ink and paper and a few good ideas.

Calligraphy can be simple or more detailed. It depends on the effect you want to create — something straightforward and clear, or a more decorative and intricate style.

When your family are sending letters ask to address the envelopes. You will impress the person who receives the letter. Some people even save the envelopes.

You will see how to form the different calligraphy styles in more detail later but for now let's try to get a feel for this magical writing art.

MATERIALS

Here are the materials you will need to start off. Most of them can be bought from an art supplies shop.

WHAT DO I WRITE WITH?

A pen with a broad nib used with ink is the most common tool to use. Here are the different types:

■ STEEL NIBS IN PEN-HOLDERS

These are not very expensive and last a long time if you look after them. The nibs come in different widths. Use a separate pen for each colour ink you use.

■ CARTRIDGE CALLIGRAPHY PEN SET

These sets have a pen, some cartridges containing ink for the pen, and up to six nibs.

■ DISPOSABLE CALLIGRAPHY PENS

These pens have broad fibre tips. You can get them up to three millimetres wide and in at least three strong colours. Don't press too hard with these pens or the point will bend or become blunt. Once they dry out you throw them away.

My favourite pen is a bamboo pen which I cut myself.

Get a piece of bamboo about 1 cm in diameter. Make these three cuts.

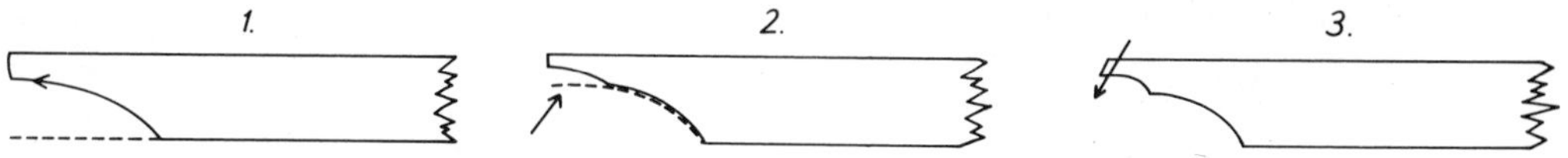

Then trim the point for width.

Ask an adult to help with the cutting as bamboo is tough. You need all your fingers for writing!

The longer you write the better it works.

It has a character all of its own.

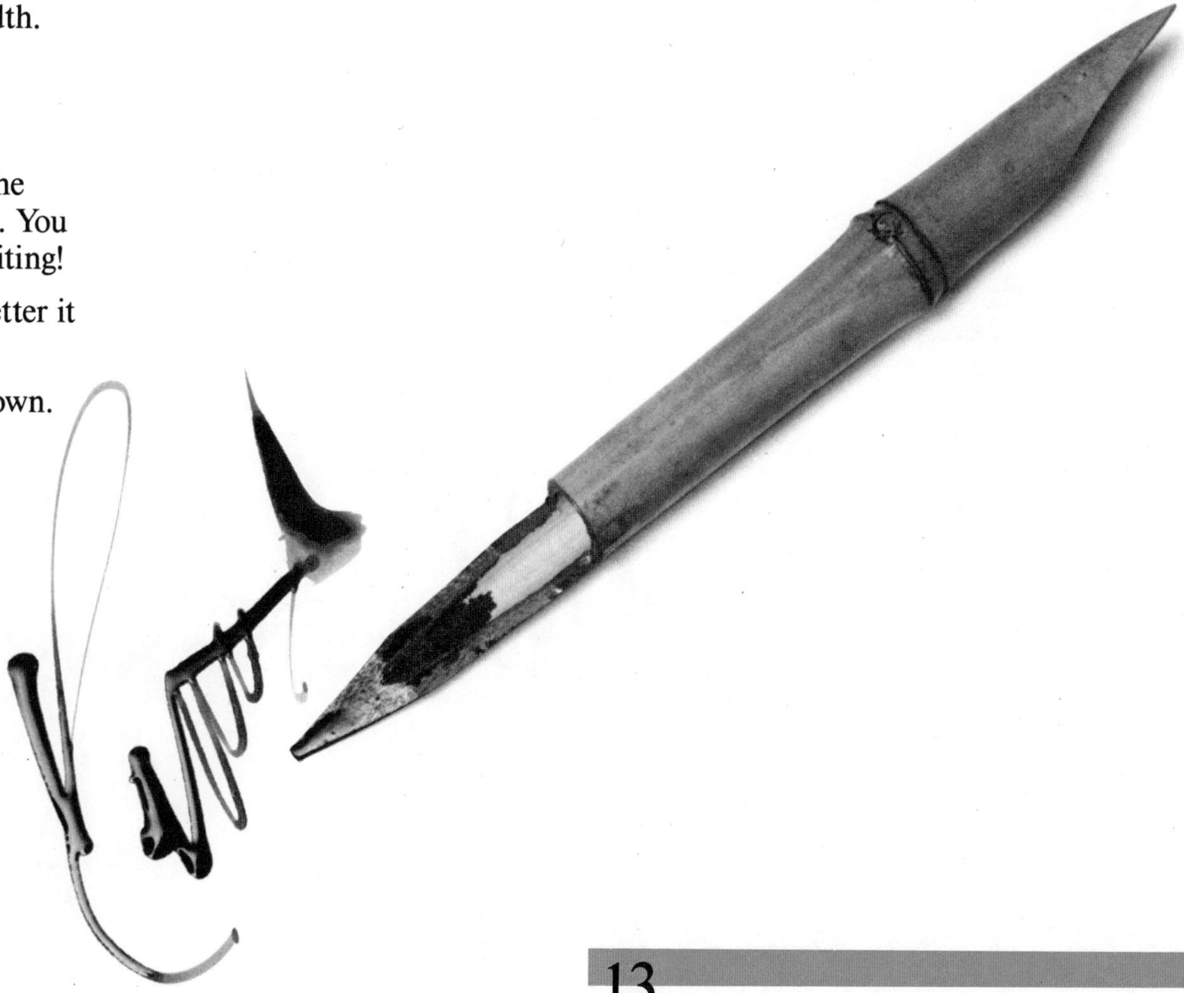

CREATE SPECIAL EFFECTS WITH AS MANY DIFFERENT PENS AS YOU CAN FIND. IT'S A CHALLENGE!

Dry brush

bamboo

bamboo

Steel Nib

MASKING

Spatter

·Outline·

bamboo

double pointed nibs

Felt-pen on tissue paper

BRUSH

EXPERIMENT WITH ALL OF THEM!

WHAT PAPER WILL I USE?

The paper must be smooth. Photocopying paper is good to start off with, or bank or bond white paper bought from the newsagent. Layout paper is also suitable.

For special work use better paper. You can use calligraphy pads of parchment, coloured paper, even handmade paper. This type of paper is more expensive so save it for special occasions. Rule guidelines on the paper with a soft 2B pencil and when the ink is dry, rub them out.

WHAT INK WILL I USE?

There are different types of ink.

Non-waterproof ink is soluble in water. It is used in fountain pens and cartridge pens so that they won't clog up. It comes in black, blue, blue-black and red. Use black ink when you start off as it is less expensive and good for practice. It washes off fingers and clothes fairly easily but take care using it — no ink is easy to remove completely.

Waterproof inks are permanent. They come in bright, strong colours but are expensive so save them for special work.

Gouache is a water-soluble poster colour which usually comes in a tube. Mix it with a little water until it is like cream. Use a soft brush to put the paint onto a nib in a pen holder. With gouache you can mix any colour, tone or shade.

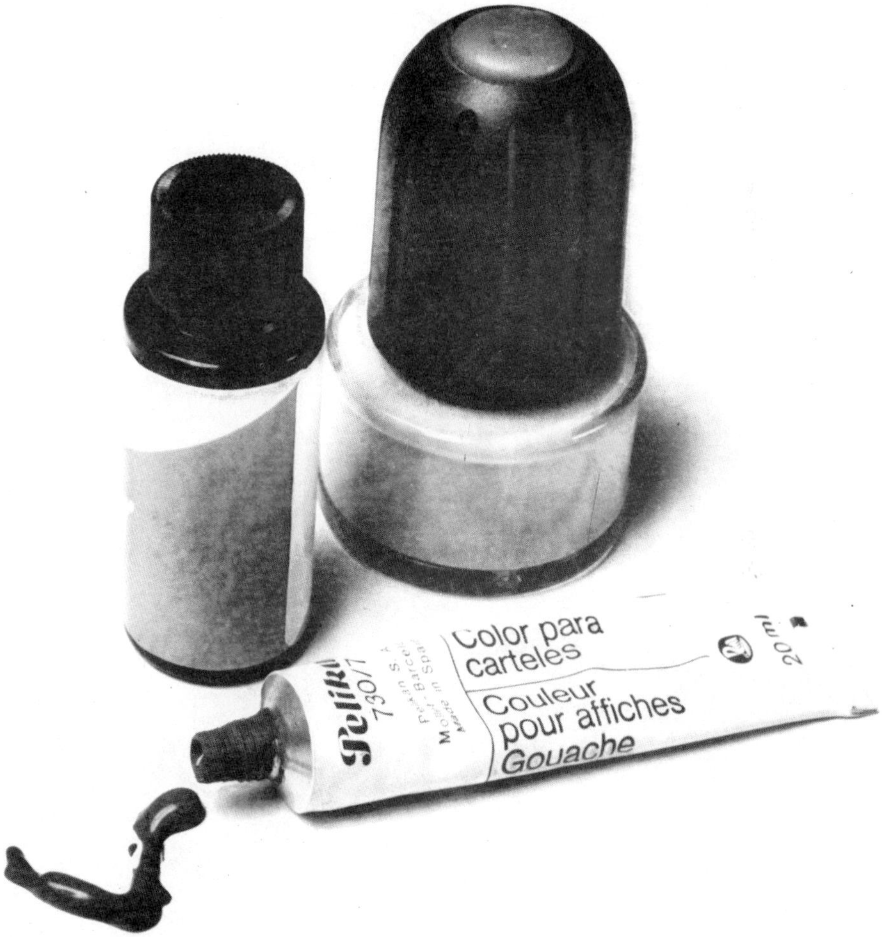

WHERE DO I BEGIN?

Start by loosening up your pen movements. Follow these patterns and experiment with the pen.

How many different widths can you create with the pen? Does the ink have to be solid colour?

Try holding the pen at different angles. What different effects can you create?

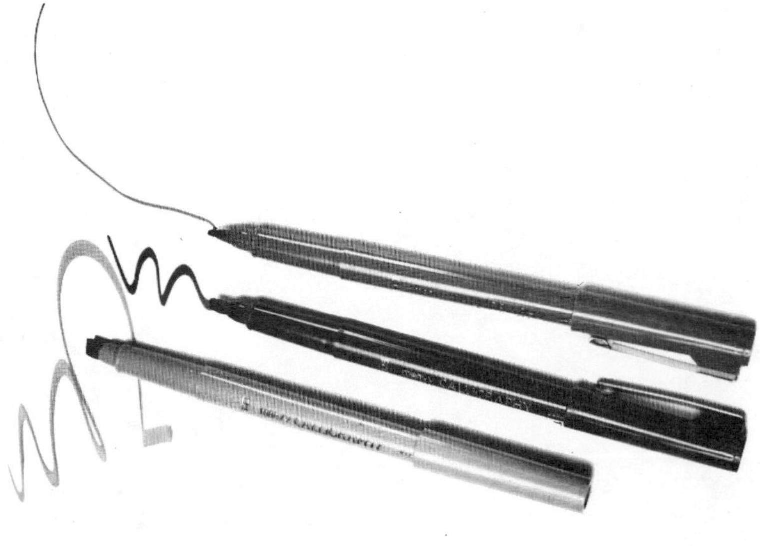

Once you have a feel for the pen you need to hold it at the correct angle. By now you will have noticed that the angle of the nib affects the width of the strokes.

HOW SHOULD I HOLD THE PEN?

Hold it lightly and with the nib hitting the page at 45 degrees.

Remember to keep this angle the same as you move across the page. Once you've found your grip play around with some of these strokes. Follow the arrows and remember — keep the nib at 45 degrees!

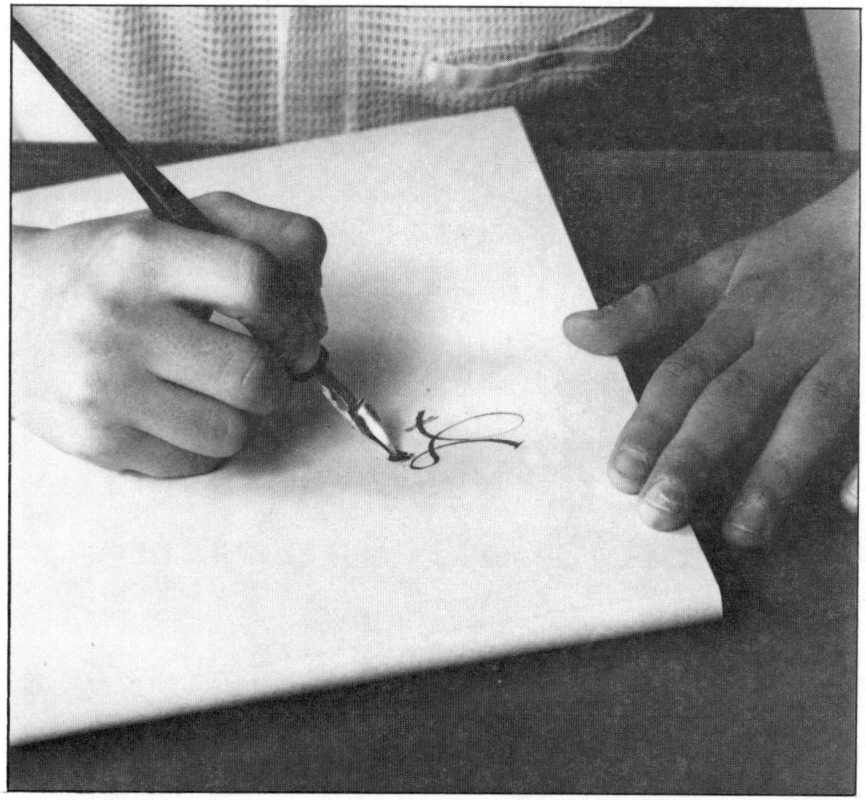

NOTICE THE CHANGE IN WIDTH AT DIFFERENT POINTS

THE CHANGE IN THE WIDTH OF THE STROKES MAKES YOUR WRITING ATTRACTIVE. TRY THESE:

Use your pen freely on practice paper. Make up your own patterns.

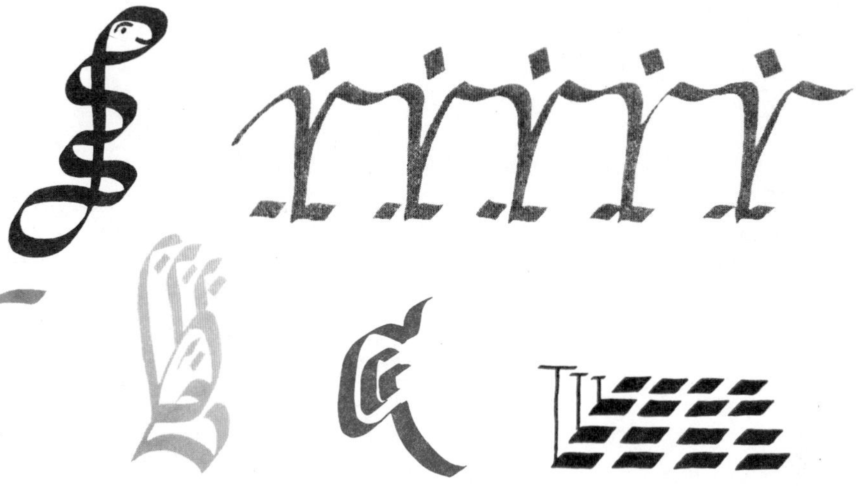

WHEN YOU FEEL COMFORTABLE CONTROLLING YOUR PEN TRY WRITING WITH IT IN YOUR NORMAL HANDWRITING.

Sing a song of sixpence,
A pocket full of rye,
Four-and-twenty blackbirds
Baked in a pie.

Remember to rinse your nibs after you use them to remove all the ink. Dry them with a soft cotton cloth and keep them away from moisture.

Get to know the owner of your local art supply shop and what they sell. Experiment with different materials. Your art supply shop is a gold mine for the future!

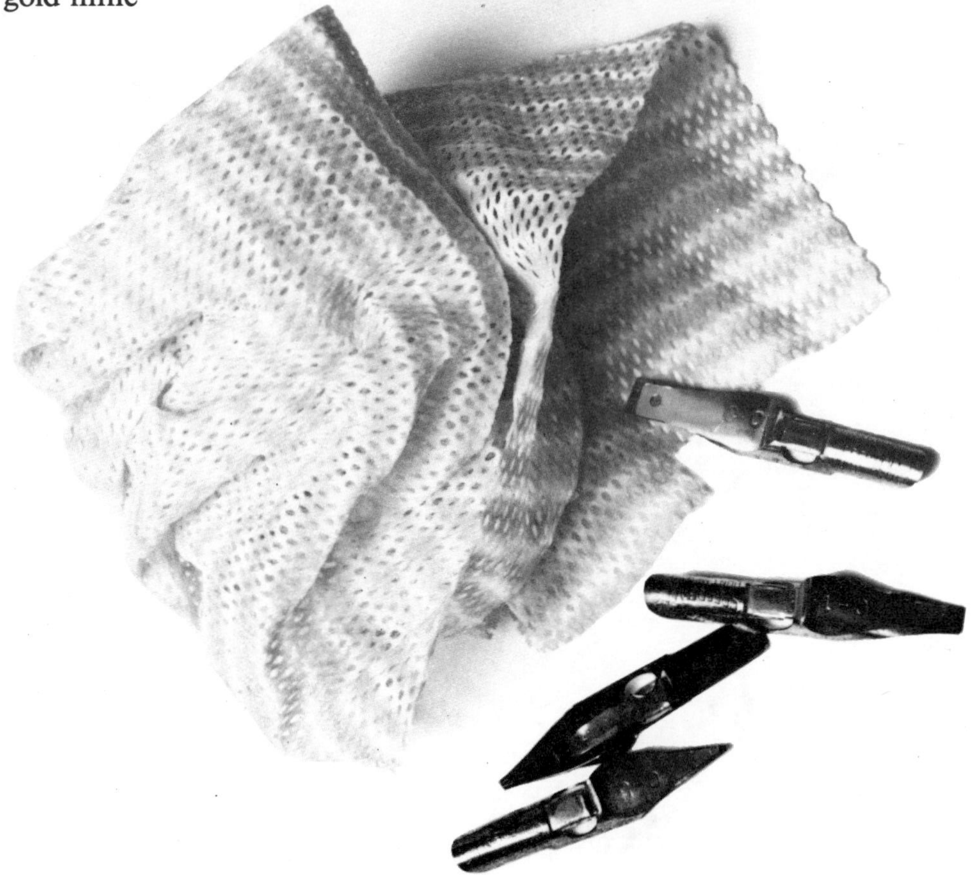

LEFT-HANDED OR RIGHT- HANDED?

If you were growing up hundreds of years ago and you wrote with your left hand people would have thought you were definitely touched by evil. Even fifty years ago you would have been considered a little odd because you chose to write with your left hand. These days people have finally come to their senses and realised that, whether left-handed or right-handed, a person's character is not affected by their handwriting preference.

WHAT IF I'M RIGHT-HANDED?

Put the paper in front of you and tilt it a little to your left. This way when your pen meets the paper it should write at a 45 degree angle. Try to point the pen up your forearm towards your elbow.

Before you settle completely, find a comfortable position for you and your paper. Relax your hand and don't grip the pen too tightly. Try to get a smooth even stroke with the pen. Don't press down on the nib or it will skid sideways.

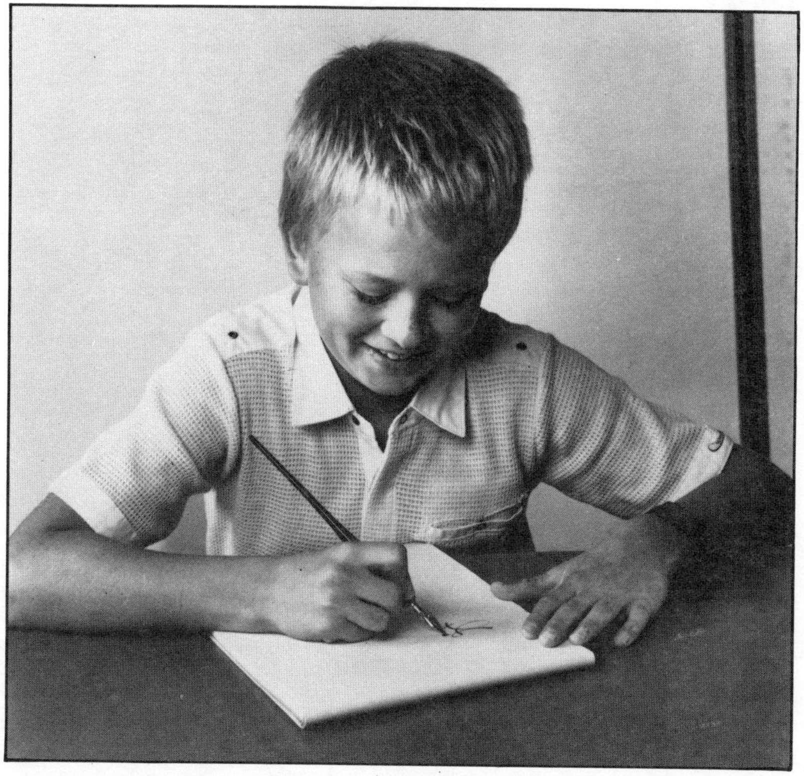

WHAT IF I'M LEFT-HANDED?

If you are left-handed, you will probably develop your own calligraphy style using slightly different methods but the end result will be the same as for right-handers.

The hardest part for you is to keep your hand below where you're writing so that you won't smudge the ink. Try using a left-handed nib which is designed to help you do this. You will have to push the nib with your fingers more than a right-hander but be careful not to press the nib into the paper or it will blot.

You may prefer to use the straight nib and to tilt the paper much more to the right so that it is almost vertical.

Whichever nib you use keep your elbow close to your side and tilt the paper to your right so that the nib meets the paper at 45 degrees. Experiment a little until you find a comfortable position and grip.

If you write with your hand over where you are writing you will need to reverse the direction of your strokes. Instead of pulling the pen you will have to push it which is not ideal. See how you go but try hard to train your hand to sit below your writing. Your results will be better in the long run.

STYLES OF CALLIGRAPHY

Different calligraphy styles have developed over hundreds of years from ancient Roman styles to the lavish Gothic styles of the Middle Ages.

Your own handwriting is a form of the simple italic style (so called because it originated in Italy). With just a few changes you will be able to write in full italic. Here's how:

FORMAL ITALIC

a b c d e e f g h i j k l m n o p q r s
t u v w x y z

A B C D E F G H I J K L M
O P Q R S T U V W X Y Z

The big change is in the capitals.

These are called *swash* capitals.

What was it that made the fox jump over the lazy dog?

This is a cursive style suitable for almost any occasion.

For very formal occasions try this unjoined italic style.

a b c d e f g h i j k l m n o p q r s t u v w x y z

The quick brown fox was very sneaky. It crept up to the sleeping dog and it jumped over him. His reputation has never recovered.

You can make these italic letters more ornate by flourishing them. To flourish you extend some strokes making a special feature of them like this:

Long buzz all Th off zoo kick

Simple Roman

This style is very round. It looks simple but be careful because every little mistake stands out clearly. Never push your pen — always pull your pen away from the ink which will keep you in control of your stroke.

abcdefghijklmnopqrst
uvwxyz

ABCDEFGHIJKLMNOP
QRSTUVWXYZ

These patterns will give you an idea of the strokes to use in the Roman style. Try them.

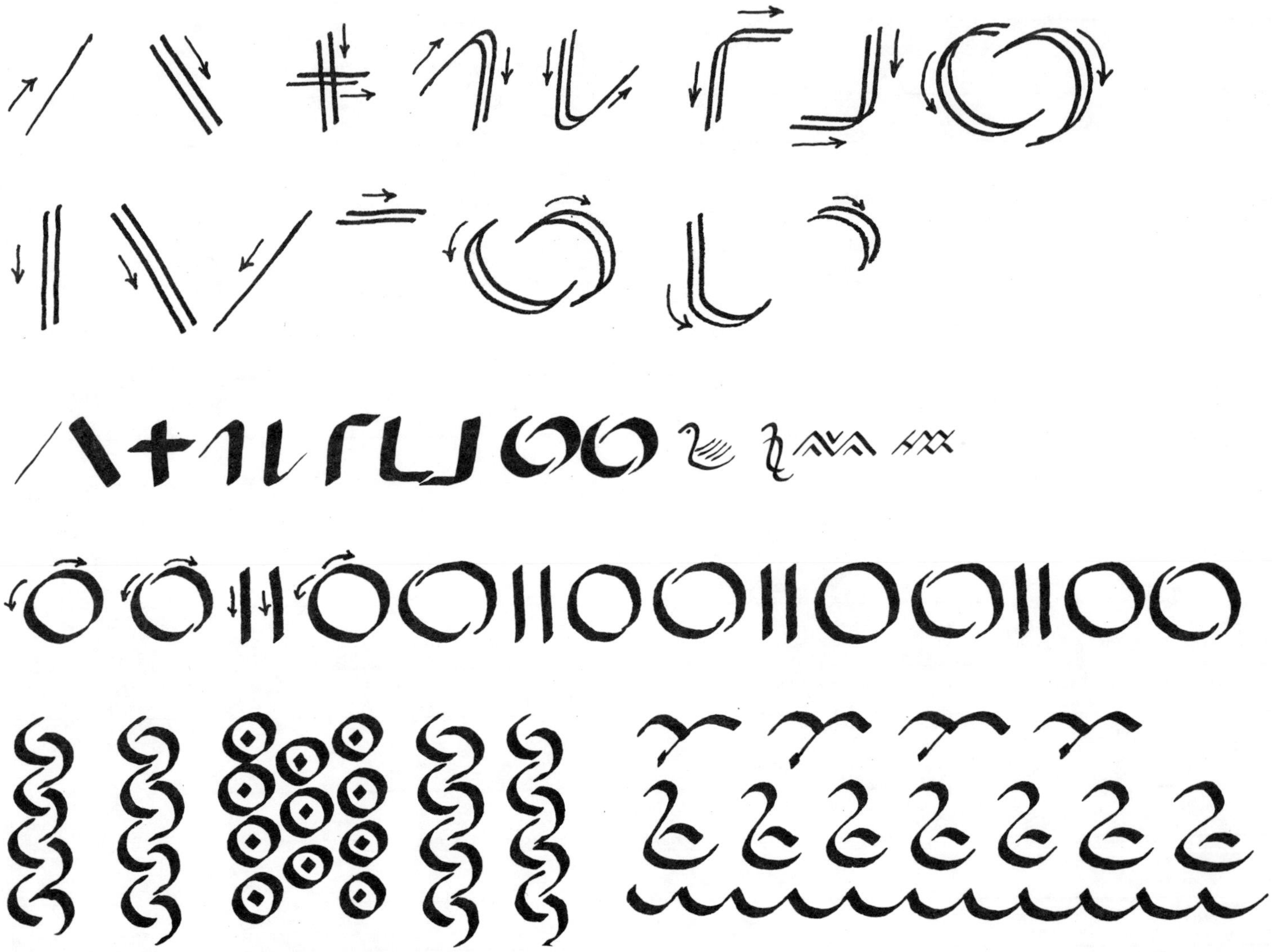

Uncial

This very old alphabet is round and fat and comfortable. The uncials take up a lot of space as most of the letters fill a square. Both uncial and Roman were originally written in upper-case only.

Follow the arrows.

half uncials

With the uncials came the first lower-case letters. These were called half uncials and they were the first step towards cursive or joined writing. If you write the letters close together they look as if they are joined.

a b c d d e f g h i j k k

l m n o p q r s t u

v w x y z

Carolingian

This style was developed by a monk called Alquin of York in the ninth century while he was trying to sort out the mixed up pages of the king's hand-written books. The name Carolingian came from the group of kings reigning at that time, the Carolingian kings.

Think of a circle when you are writing this style. Let it spread out and take up room. There is a slight slope. The tall letters are at least two small letters high. Use uncials for capitals with this style. Carolingian introduces serifs, or caps on the tips of some of the letters.

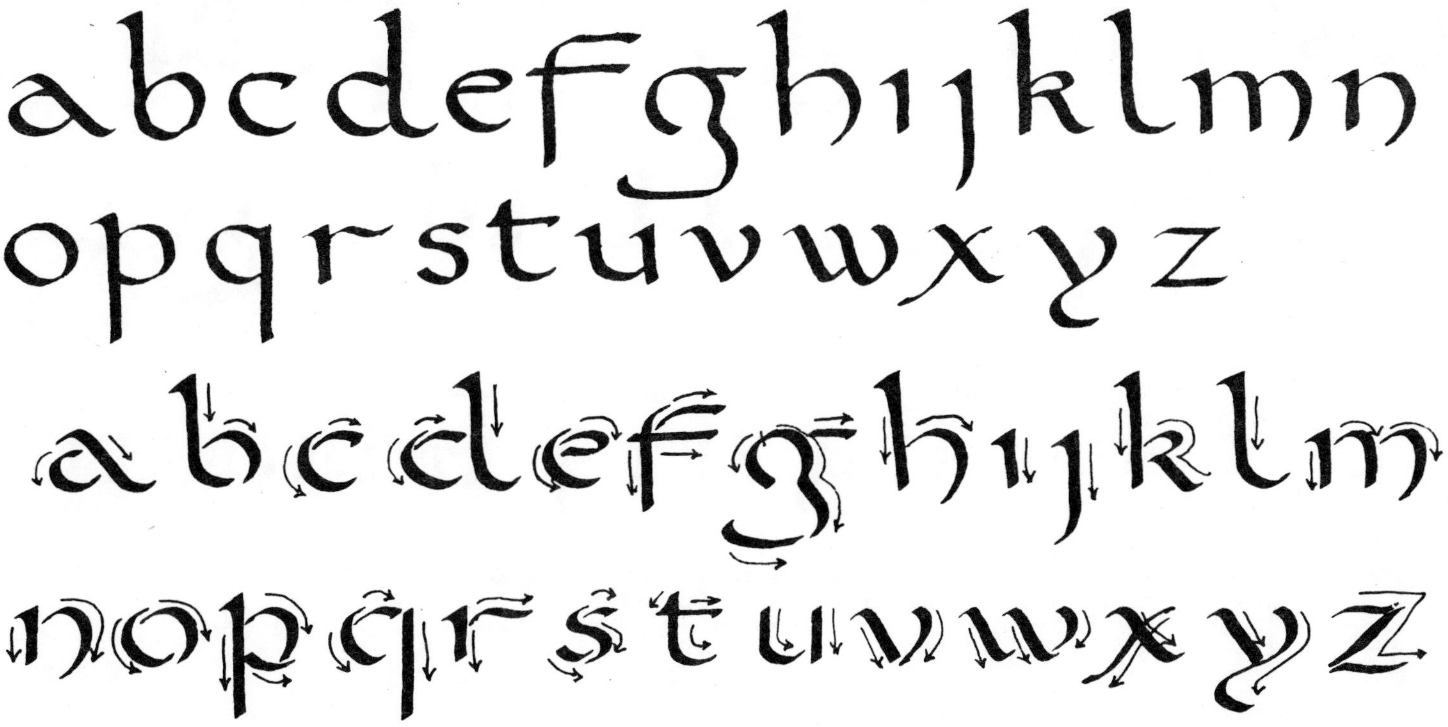

Gothic ~ Black Letter ~

This style was developed because there was a paper shortage and uncial and Carolingian took up too much space. Gothic letters were also easier to carve into printing blocks when printing books.

It's the style we all want to be able to write in but remember it can be hard to read. The lower-case letters are written with straight strokes; there is no slope. Make each stroke deliberate, separate and crisp.

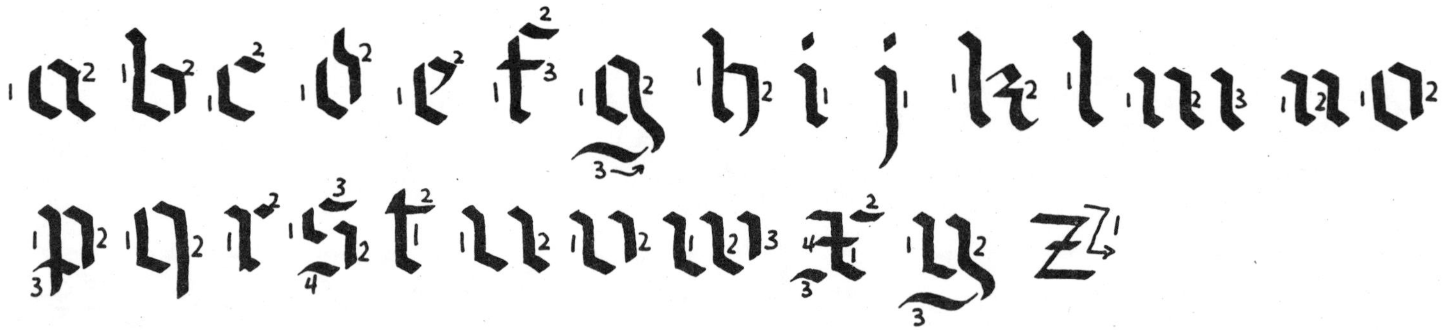

Never write anything just in capitals.
It's almost impossible to read.

WHAT DO YOU THINK?

As well as showing you how the letters are formed these fractured letters look interesting. Try them.

The letters should be written close together, with about a nib-width between the words.

a b c d e f g h i j k l m

n o p q r s t u v w x y z

A B C D E F G H I J K L M N

O P Q R S T U V W X Y Z

Here is a more elaborate set of capitals.

A B C D E F G H I J K L M

N O P Q R S T U V W X Y Z

The Pointed Serif

You can extend some of these styles by using the pointed serif at the end of some letters. Carolingian uses them to dress up a lot of the letters.

MAKE A SERIF LIKE THIS:

1 Slide the nib on its edge for one pen's width.

2 With a circular motion return to the sidestroke.

3 Complete the downstroke from the top.

Don't be afraid of it. It works.

WHERE TO USE THE SERIF

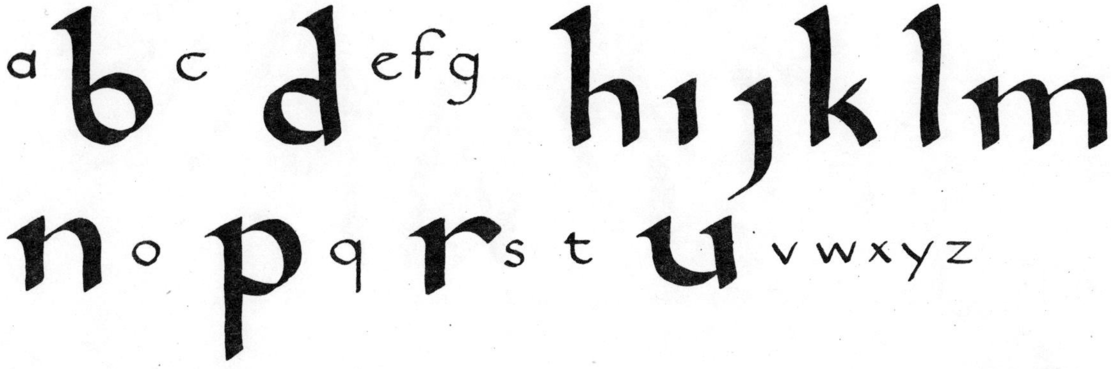

ORGANISING THE PAGE

Spacing is very important. Decide what you want to write and then plan how you are going to fit it onto the page.

How many lines will you need?

How far apart will the lines be?

Will all the writing be in straight lines?

Will all the lines start at the same point? End at the same point?

Can you fit the writing inside a shape?

How much paper will you leave bare?

What style of writing will you use?

Every minute you spend preparing will make the final product easier to create and better in appearance.

Experiment with different nib sizes and letter heights.

incredible incredible incredible incredible

Have a reason for changing the normal look of the letters.

Do you want a word to stand out?

Will the look of the page reflect a feeling, a description, a mental image?

Take care with the spacing of letters in a word. It should look even.

intelligent intelligent intelligent

Often thin letters such as *i* and *l* need less space than rounder letters such as *a* and *w* .

VERSALS

Versals are decorated capital letters which you can use to give a stunning start to a poem, story or paragraph. Here are some examples.

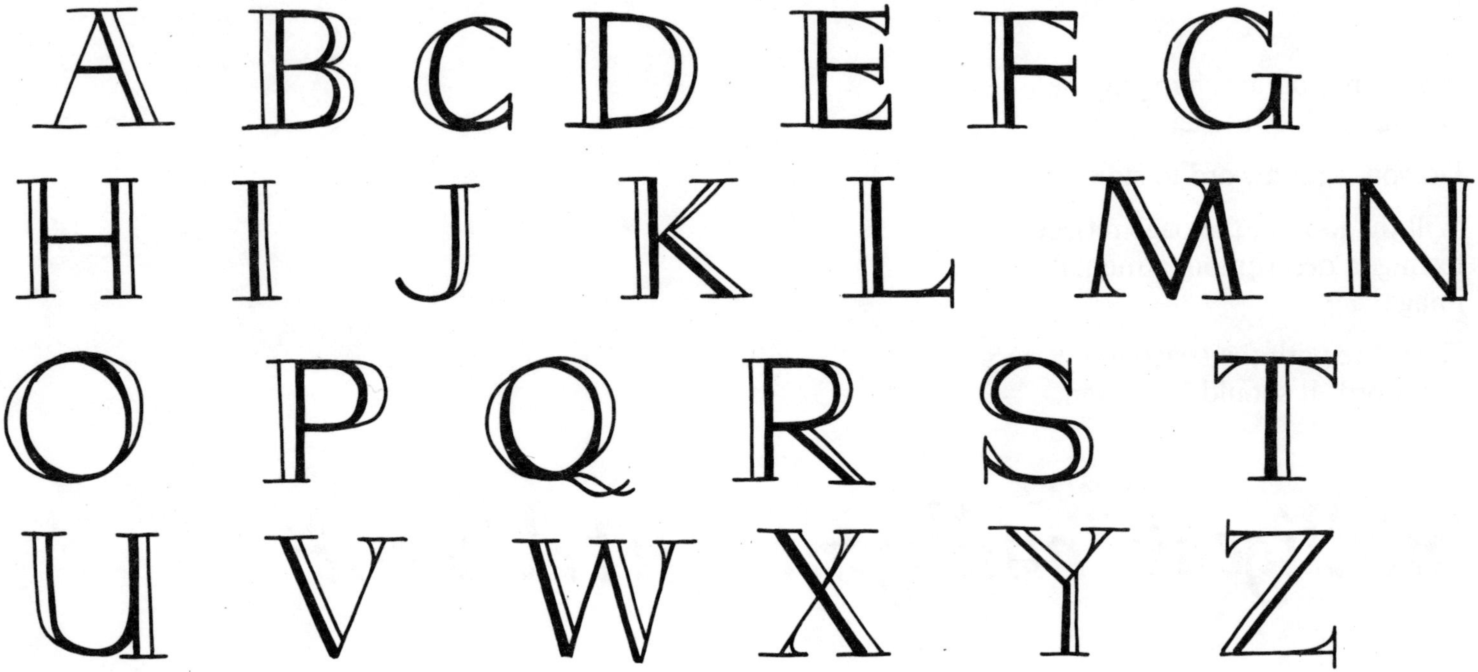

As a general rule you add the extra strokes to the outside of the letter.

You can leave them open or fill them in.

Here is a more ornate set drawn inside squares.

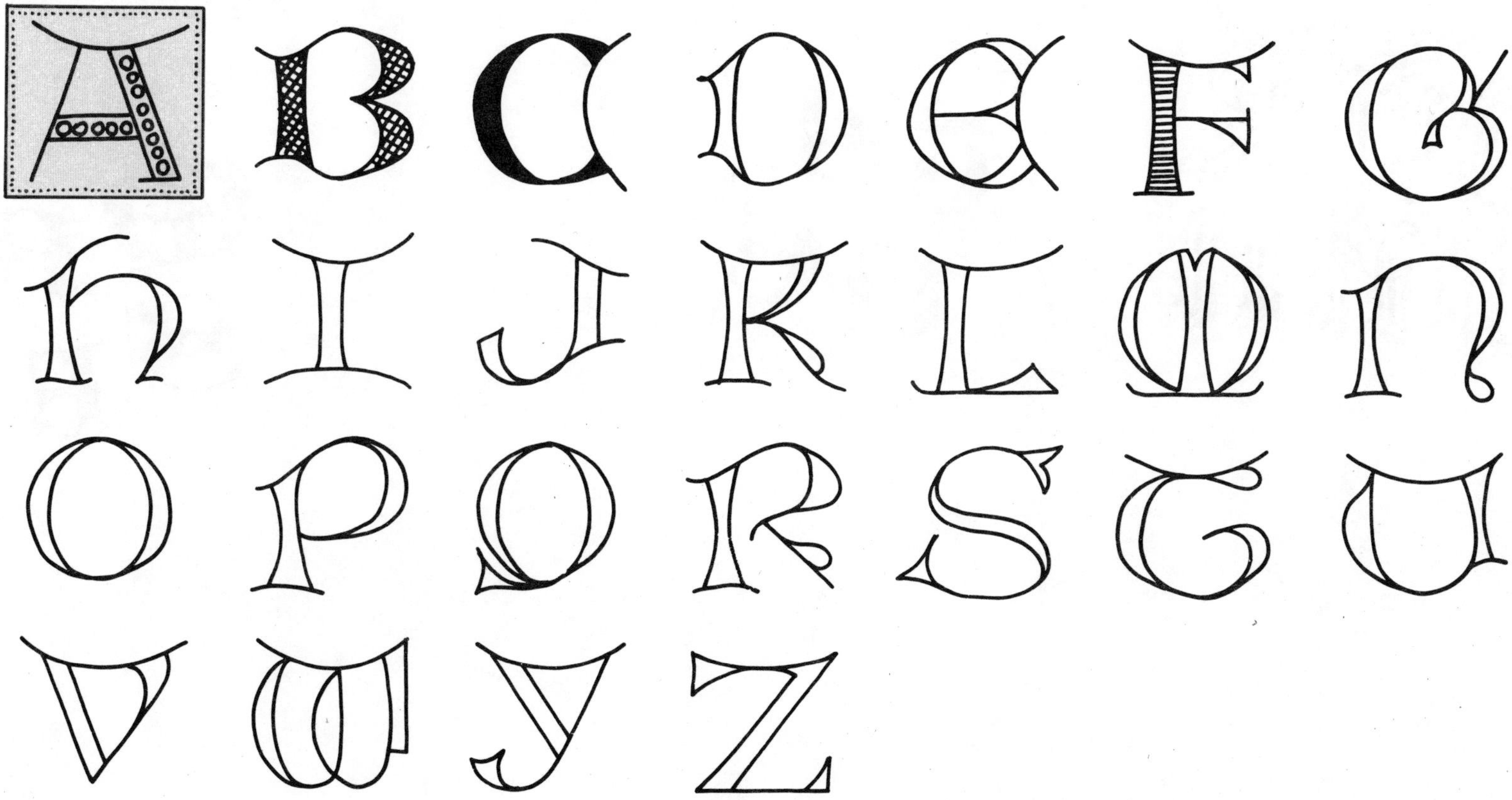

CREATE AS YOU GO.

abc
defg
hijk
lmn

Ahakendqlf

TA
NE

MB
SF

Create

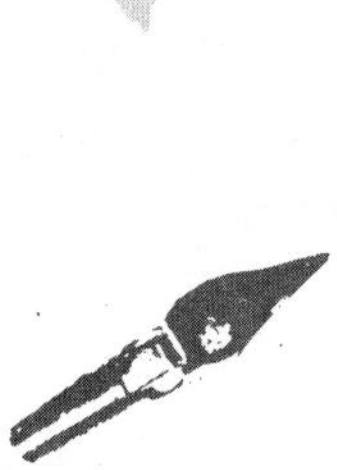

the storm

BEAUTIFUL HANDWRITING EVERY DAY

Now that you have tried your hand at some of the more decorative styles of writing you will no doubt be more interested in your own handwriting style. It is easy to see that many of the styles used in calligraphy are an extension of the handwriting you are learning.

The best way to master calligraphy is to follow the letter formations, remember a few simple rules and practise a little each day. If you do the same with your own handwriting you will develop a beautiful style for every day!

You can be creative with your handwriting practice. It doesn't have to be long and boring. Create patterns out of letter shapes and work with a variety of materials. Sometimes it's fun to use huge sheets of paper and big crayons, or try practising on a chalkboard.

The next few pages will show you the fun way to improve your handwriting. This style is a simple form of italic and is easy to learn as the hand movements follow the natural flow of your hand. Use the ideas as a guide and relax into your own natural style.

Dear Dave
can you come to
my party?

FINDING YOUR OWN SLOPE

Your writing should slope a little to the right. Tilt the paper a little to the left, put both elbows on the desk and scribble in the top right-hand corner of the page moving your hand up and down like this:

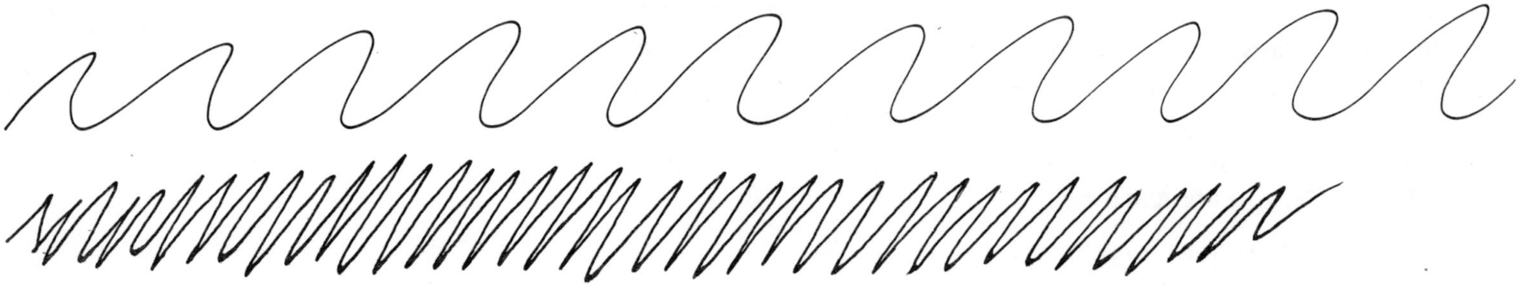

These scribbles will show you the natural slope your hand wants to write at. From now on concentrate on that slope every time your pen is moving downwards. Follow your own slope. Your downstroke will decide how even your writing will be. It is the key movement in your handwriting.

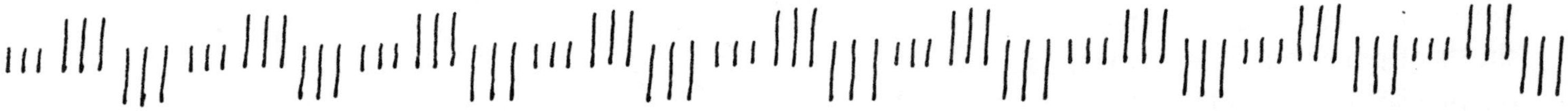

TWO BASIC LETTER PATTERNS

Let's look at the letters and how they are formed.

If you join a row of downstrokes without lifting your pen there are only two ways to do it:

1

2

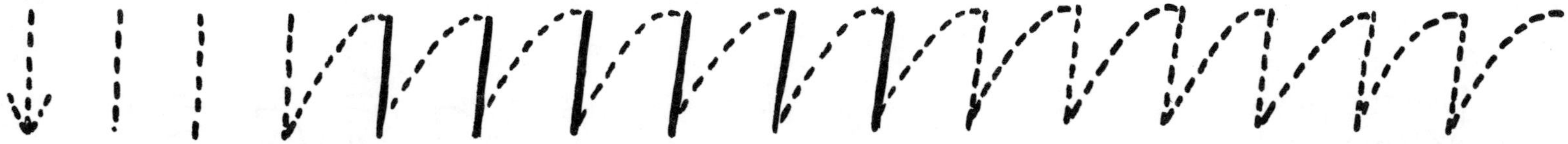

Try these patterns. Every letter of the alphabet is hidden in them.

LETTERS FROM PATTERN 1

Using the downstroke:

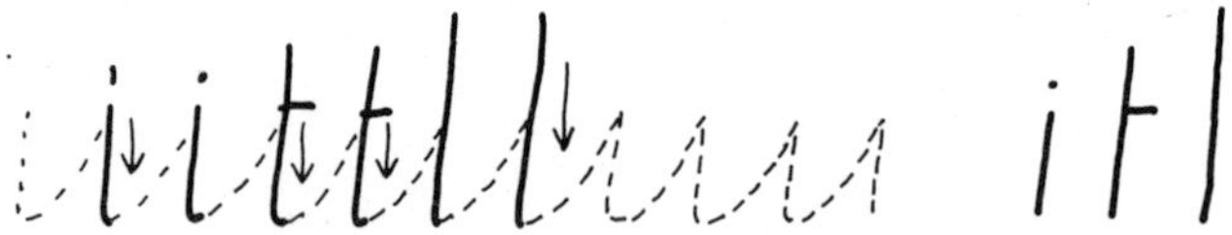

Using the downstroke and push stroke:

Now add the upward curve.

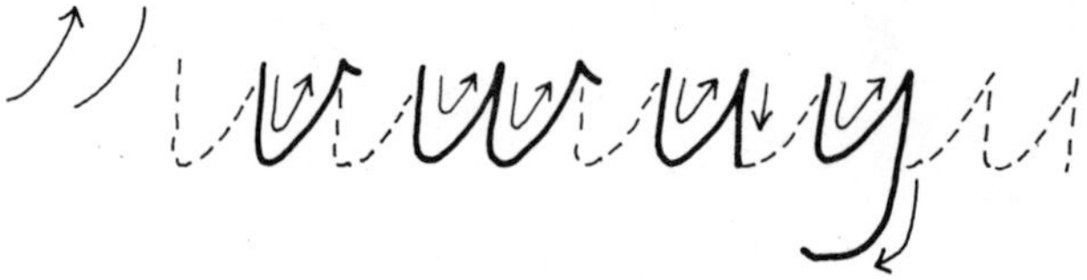

Use the push stroke as a starting stroke.

The *e* starts with an upstroke.

The *s* is a push-pull-push stroke without stopping.

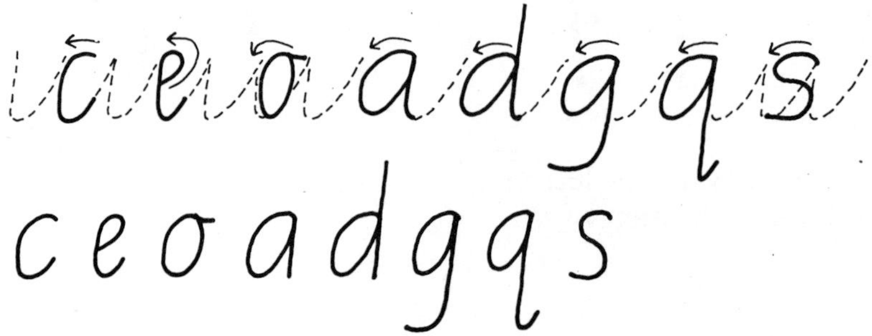

These wedge shapes are formed from making the sharp turn at the top of each curve. Make sure they are there and that you do not do zig-zags when you form the curves.

COMPLETING THE ALPHABET

If you look at the second pattern you will see that it uses just one new stroke: 

Using all the strokes you can now complete the alphabet.

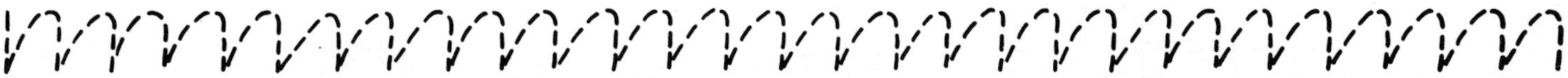

These are the script or printed letters. They are unjoined.

i t l f j v w u y c e o a d g q s n m r h k b p x z

Try out these letters before you go on to cursive or joined writing.

uiiuiiuiiuii uiiuiiuiiuiiuiiuii uiiuiiuiiuiiuiiuiiuiiuii

mcmamemomumsmimnmrmvmwmxmzmcmamemo

dpdgdqdjdydpdgdqdjdydpdgdqdjdydpdgdqdjdy

stslsdsbshskstslsdsbshskstslsdsbshskstslsdsbs

dbdb db dbdb dbdbdbdbdb dbdbdbdbdbdbdbdbdb

mxmxmxmxmx mxmxmx mxmxmx mxmxmxmxmx

hyhyhyhyhyhyhyhyhyhyhyhyhyhyhyhyh

stsststsststsststsststsststsststsststsststssts

lelelelelelelelelelelelelelelelelelelelelel

aqaqaqaqaqaqaqaqaqaqaqaqaq

ststststststststststststststst

fjfjfjfjfjfjfjfjfjfjfjfjfjfjf

orororororororororororororororo

cmcmcmcmcmcmcmcmcmcmcmcmcmcmcmcmcmcmcmcmcm

mmmmmmmmmmmmmmmmm

ieleieieieieieieieieieieieieieieieieiei

aaauaaauaaauaaauaaauaa

fjjfjjfjjfjjfjjfjjfjjfjjfjjfjjfjjfjjfjjfjjfj

xzxzxzxzxzxzxzxzxzxz

vwvwvwvwvwvwvwvwvwvw

njnjnjnjnjnjnjnjnjnjnjnjn

bgbgbgbgbgbgbgbgbgbgb

hkhkhkhkhkhkhkhkh

vhyvhyvhyvhyvhyvhyvh

dpdpdpdpdpdpdpdpdpdp

x·x·x·x·x·x·x·x·x·x·x·x·x·x·x·x·x·x·x·x·x·x

umumumumumumumumumumum

bybybybybybybybybybyb

wiiwiiwiiwiiwiiwiiwiiwiiwiiwiiwiiwii

CAPITALS

Straight lines only:

ILTHFEKAVWNMXYZ

Straight lines and curves:

PDBRJU

ROUNDED CAPITALS

CGOQS

WASHINGTON CANBERRA
LONDON WELLINGTON

Capitals should slope and should not be any taller than one-and-a-half lower letter heights. Don't make them too tall and thin.

Slope with some capitals can be tricky.

JOINED WRITING

Once you feel confident with the script letters have a look at these cursive letters. Notice the entry and exit strokes, or the strokes which start and finish each letter.

The letters are almost the same as the script letters except for the extra strokes which join the letters together.

i u v w j y f t l c e a d g q o s

n m r h k b p x z

First try writing this sentence in cursive letters without joining them.

Mary had a little lamb its fleece was white as snow.

Now fill in the gaps with the entry and exit strokes and you'll see how the letters join together.

Mary had a little lamb.

THE JOINS

There are four types of joins.

THE WHOLE JOIN

in um ar di nu

Any letter which ends with an exit stroke can be joined to any letter that starts with an entry stroke.

a d h i k l m n t e u x

These letters have exit strokes.

i j m n r p u v w x y z

These letters have entry strokes.

The whole join is the most common.

THE HORIZONTAL JOIN

ow ru vi wa to os

This join needs a little dip

ow not ow

THE CHOICE JOIN

When joining a letter to one with no entry stroke, write the second letter to touch the previous exit stroke.

ad na ca ic ug

You choose whether or not to lift your pen between letters.

go ju ye qu pa bi so

THE NO-JOIN

Lift your pen after *g j y q z p b* and *s*. Once you're confident with forming *p b* and *s* you can join them.

pen but so public assist

When in doubt, lift your pen.

Don't join *e* to *r o w v* or *x*.

Write slowly, smoothly and rhythmically. Remind yourself of the elements of good writing as you work.

These joins are fun but they are different.

ta ti tu to tn th fi fs ffi fa

as is os essi exi oxe axe ixi

uz ozz iz uzz or uzz maze

CHECK!

Are your upstrokes fine?

Are your turns smooth?

Are your downstrokes parallel?

Relax, do not press hard.

Use the pen as you would a brush.

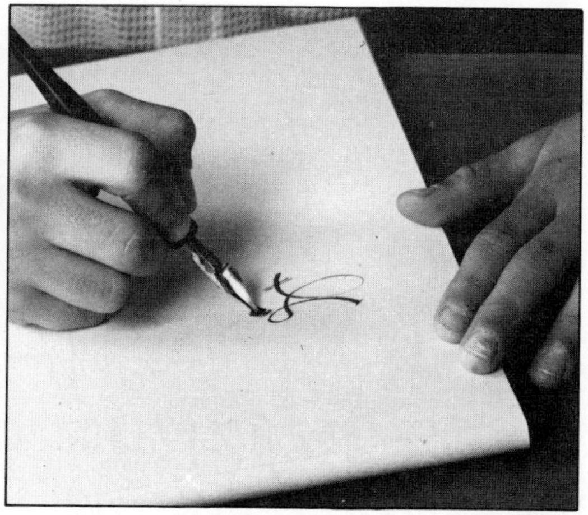

Exercises for Cursive Writing

lililililililililililililililililililililililililililililililililil

fufufufufufufufufufufufufufufufufufufufufufufu

utututututututututututututututututututututututututututututut

cecececececececececececececececececececececececececececececece

ododododododododododododododododododododo

agagagagagagagagagagagagagagagagagaga

xcxcxcxcxcxcxcxcxcxcxcxcxcxcxcxcxcxcxc

rsrsrsrsrsrsrsrsrsrsrsrsrsrsrsrsrsrsrs

vwvwvwvwvwvwvwvwvwvwvwvwvwvwvwvwvwvwvw

lmlmlmlmlmlmlmlmlmlmlmlmlmlmlmlml

azazazazazazazazazazazazazazazazazazazaz

sisisisisisisisisisisisisisisisisisisisisisisisisisisisis

ftftftftftftftftftftftftftftftftftftftftftftftft

okokokokokokokokokokokokokokokokok

bebebebebebebebebebebebebebebebebebebebebeb

oyoyoyoyoyoyoyoyoyoyoyoyoyoyoyoyoyoyoy

npnpnpnpnpnpnpnpnpnpnpnpnpnpnpnpnpnp

Avoid making mistakes by planning carefully

Mark out your layout
Work out the balance of the page in pencil
Know where you want to use colour

Take your time

A B C D E F G H I K L
M N O P Q R S T U V
W X Y Z Z

abcdefghijklmn
opqrstuvwxyz

So that's it. An easy way to develop beautiful handwriting. Use the letter shapes as decoration for borders, for creating funny pictures or for background patterns. Your practice can be as creative as your imagination will allow.

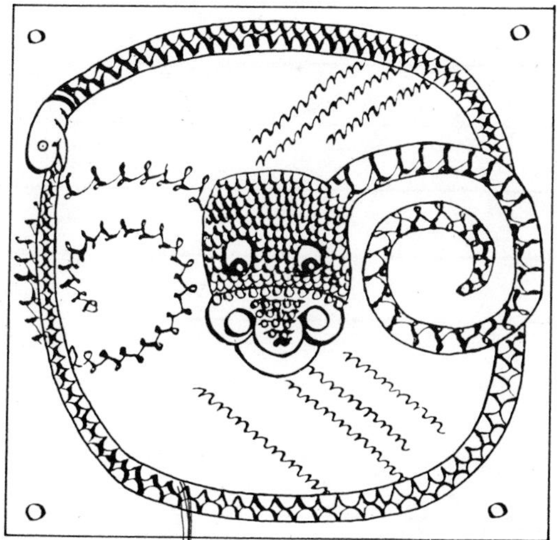

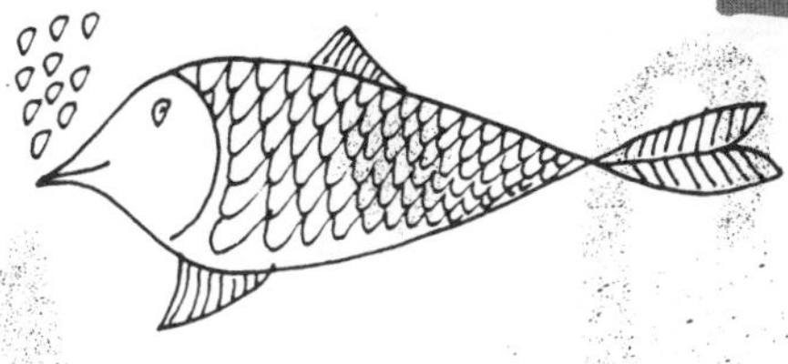

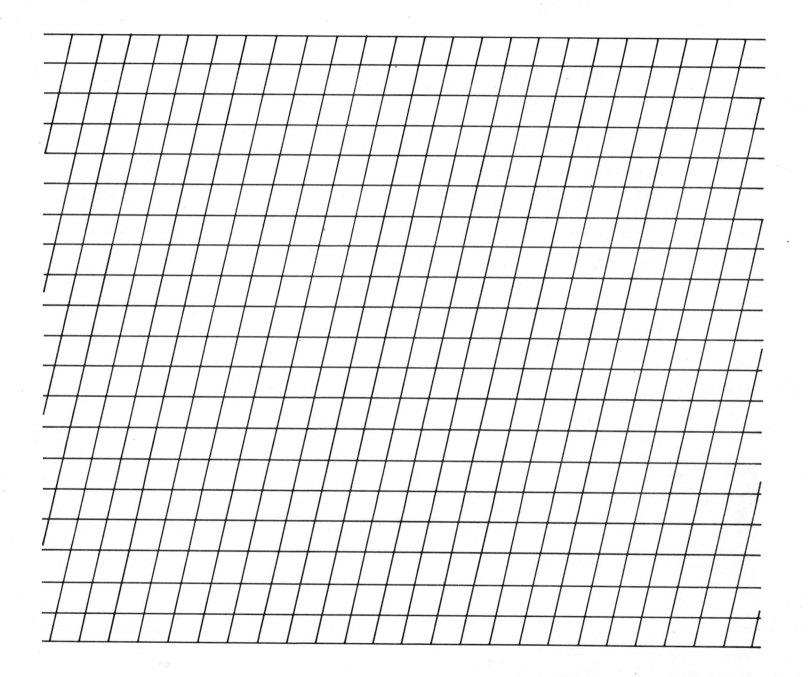